Cracking the Code: Becoming a Top Technical Recruiter

A Step-by-Step Guide

By Jon D. McClain

PUBLISHED BY: J. McClain

Copyright © 2024, 2025 All Rights Reserved

No part of this publication may be copied, reproduced in any format, by any means, electronic or otherwise without the prior consent from the Publisher and copyright owner of this book.

Table of Contents

Preface

- Introduction to Technical Recruiting
- Author's Background and Expertise
- Why This Book Will Help You Succeed

Chapter 1: The Recruiter's Dilemma – Why Make the Switch?

Subtitle: Exploring the "Why" Behind Technical Recruiting

- The Growing Demand for Tech Talent
- Unique Challenges of Technical Recruiting
- Future-Proofing Your Career

Chapter 2: Decoding the Tech Industry – What You Must Know

Subtitle: Understanding the Technical Landscape

- Key Sectors in the Tech Industry
- Basic Tech Terminology and Tools
- Emerging Trends and Industry Players

Chapter 3: Bridging the Gap – How to Build Tech Fluency

Subtitle: Learning to Speak the Language of Engineers

- Mastering the Tech Stack
- Self-Learning Resources for Recruiters
- Effective Interview Techniques for Engineers

Chapter 4: Reprogramming Your Pitch – Positioning Yourself as a Tech Recruiter

Subtitle: Branding Yourself in the Tech Recruiting Space

- Crafting a Tech-Focused Resume
- Optimizing LinkedIn for Tech Recruiting
- Showcasing Your Expertise Through Content

Chapter 5: The Recruiter's Toolkit – Mastering Platforms and Tools

Subtitle: Navigating GitHub, Stack Overflow, and Other Platforms

- Leveraging GitHub to Assess Developer Skills
- Finding Problem-Solvers on Stack Overflow
- Mastering Technical Assessments and Coding Challenges

Chapter 6: Cultivating Connections – Building Relationships with Tech Talent

Subtitle: The Human Element Behind Technical Recruiting

- Engaging Passive and Active Candidates
- Building Trust Through Transparent Communication
- Nurturing Long-Term Candidate Relationships

Chapter 7: The Hiring Manager Partnership – Aligning Expectations

Subtitle: How to Build Trust and Deliver the Right Candidates

- Understanding the Hiring Manager's Needs
- Managing Expectations and Setting Realistic Goals
- Collaborating on a Customized Interview Process

Chapter 8: Seamless Onboarding – Setting Technical Talent Up for Success

Subtitle: From Offer Acceptance to Full Integration

- The Importance of Pre-Boarding and Preparation
- Collaborating with HR for a Smooth Transition
- Making a Positive Impact on Day One

Chapter 9: Measuring Success – Key Metrics for Technical Recruiting

Subtitle: Tracking Metrics and Demonstrating Your Value

- Time-to-Hire and Quality of Hire
- Source of Hire and Offer Acceptance Rate
- Communicating Your Impact with Data

Chapter 10: The Future of Technical Recruiting – Staying Ahead

Subtitle: Continuous Learning and Emerging Trends

- Lifelong Learning in Tech Recruiting

- Key Trends Shaping the Future: AI, Remote Work, DEI
- Becoming a Thought Leader in Technical Recruiting

Final Thoughts: What's Next?
- Continuous Improvement and Staying Ahead
- Next Steps for Your Tech Recruiting Journey

Appendices
- Recommended Resources and Tools
- Glossary of Tech Terms

The Ultimate Job Hunter's Toolkit for Aspiring Technical Recruiters
Your Go-To Guide for Job Boards, Networking Communities, Certifications, and Career Opportunities in Tech Recruiting

Space for Personal Notes and To Do's

Preface

Hello, and welcome to what could be one of the most exciting steps in your career journey!

Whether you're an experienced recruiter looking to specialize, brand new to recruiting, or even someone who's never recruited before, this book is designed to set you on the path to becoming a successful Technical Recruiter or Sourcer. The world of technical recruiting is unique, challenging, and incredibly rewarding. Why? Well, for starters, technical recruiters often earn significantly more than general recruiters due to the complexity and high demand for tech talent. Depending on your region and skillset, technical recruiters can make anywhere from 20-30% more than their non-tech counterparts. On average, seasoned technical recruiters can expect salaries ranging from $85,000 to over $140,000 per year, with additional bonuses and incentives.

And let's talk about timing. Even though tech hiring may feel slow right now, the industry is once again gearing up for a resurgence. A major comeback is on the horizon, and companies will need skilled technical recruiters to source and hire the next wave of talent. The hiring landscape is shifting, and those who are prepared will be in high demand — and paid top dollar — for their expertise.

In this book, I'll guide you through the entire process of transitioning into or starting a career in technical recruiting. You'll learn everything from understanding complex technical roles to communicating effectively with engineers at all levels, data scientists, and tech leaders. These skills will not only make you more competitive in the job market but will also give you the confidence to tackle the challenges of tech recruiting head-on. By the end of this book, you'll be well-equipped and ready to thrive in this field, whether you're transitioning from general recruiting or starting fresh.

Why listen to me? I've walked the walk. As a Senior Recruiter, Senior Tech Recruiter, and Lead Recruiter, I've successfully recruited for multi-billion-dollar Corporations in various industries. I've built, led, and managed recruitment teams, trained over 60 Recruiters and Recruiting Coordinators in the United States and Canada, and consistently exceeded hiring targets throughout my career. I've worked in both corporate and academic environments, overseeing large recruitment efforts, managing significant hiring budgets, and streamlining systems. As a Senior Technical Recruiter Sourcer, I specialized in hiring senior-level engineers for high-impact teams, consistently meeting or exceeding sourcing and hiring metrics in highly competitive landscapes.

I've seen firsthand how mastering Technical Recruiting can be a career game-changer. My own journey took me from working as a volunteer worker at an international non-profit, to leading national hiring initiatives for large corporations — where I broke company records for hires — to becoming a sought-after technical recruiter at one of the most prominent names in tech. I've built diverse candidate pipelines, refined recruitment strategies, and learned what it takes to thrive in this space.

So, whether you're aiming to increase your income, pivot into a more specialized role, or learn the ropes from scratch, this book is for you. You're about to gain the insights and strategies to navigate tech hiring, build strong relationships with hiring managers and candidates, and ultimately become a go-to technical recruiter.

Congratulations on taking this step — your journey to becoming a technical recruiter has officially begun! ***Let's dive in and get started!***

Jon D. McClain

This structured guidebook will progressively take you the reader, from merely considering the transition to tech recruiting, to mastering technical recruiting with actionable insights and practical strategies to land that first job and build a successful career!

Chapter 1: The Recruiter's Dilemma – Why Make the Switch?

Subtitle: Exploring the "Why" Behind Technical Recruiting

Introduction: The Evolution of Recruiting

The recruiting landscape is evolving, and so should you. If you're an experienced recruiter contemplating a shift into technical recruiting, it's crucial to understand not just the "how," but also the "why" behind this transition. This chapter delves into the compelling reasons for making the switch, exploring both the opportunities and challenges that lie ahead in the tech recruiting realm.

The Growing Demand for Tech Talent

In today's digital age, technology is the backbone of virtually every industry. From startups to Fortune 500 companies, the need for skilled tech professionals is surging. But why is this sector so critical?

- **Unprecedented Growth**: The tech industry has been expanding at a breakneck pace, driven by innovations in artificial intelligence, cloud computing, cybersecurity, and more. This rapid growth has created a continuous demand for tech talent.

- **Skills Gap**: Despite the abundance of job openings, there's a noticeable skills gap. Many organizations struggle to find qualified candidates who not only have the technical expertise but also fit culturally within their teams.

- **High Stakes**: Hiring the right tech talent is crucial as it can significantly impact a company's innovation, productivity, and overall success. This high stakes environment means that technical recruiters are more important than ever.

Beyond Resumes: The Unique Challenges of Technical Recruiting

Transitioning to technical recruiting isn't just about learning new jargon—it's about understanding and overcoming unique challenges:

- **Complexity of Roles**: Technical roles can be highly specialized, each with its own set of requirements and technologies. This complexity requires recruiters to develop a deeper understanding of various tech domains.
- **Evaluating Skills**: Assessing technical skills goes beyond traditional interviews. It involves understanding coding challenges, tech stacks, and problem-solving abilities that can be difficult for non-technical recruiters to gauge.
- **Candidate Expectations**: Tech candidates often have different expectations regarding work culture, career progression, and compensation. Navigating these expectations requires a nuanced approach that combines industry knowledge with interpersonal skills.

Future-Proofing Your Career in a Tech-Driven World

The decision to transition to technical recruiting can also be seen as a strategic move to future-proof your career:

- **High Demand for Tech Recruiters**: As the demand for tech talent grows, so does the need for skilled tech recruiters. This specialization not only opens doors to new opportunities but also positions you as an expert in a field with high growth potential.
- **Career Growth and Compensation**: Technical recruiting roles often come with attractive compensation packages and

opportunities for career advancement, reflecting the critical nature of these positions.

- **Impact and Influence**: By becoming a technical recruiter, you'll have the chance to play a pivotal role in shaping the tech industry by connecting top talent with groundbreaking projects and companies.

Conclusion: Embracing the Change

Making the switch from general recruiting to technical recruiting is not just a career move—it's a chance to be at the forefront of technological innovation. As you embark on this journey, remember that the skills you've developed as a recruiter are transferable and valuable. With the right mindset and preparation, you can leverage your existing expertise while gaining new insights and capabilities that will not only advance your career but also contribute significantly to the tech industry's growth.

In the next chapter, we'll dive into the technical landscape itself, breaking down the fundamental knowledge you'll need to succeed as a tech recruiter.

Chapter 2: Decoding the Tech Industry – What You Must Know

Subtitle: Understanding the Technical Landscape

Introduction: The World of Tech Unveiled

To transition successfully into technical recruiting, it's imperative to have a solid understanding of the tech industry. This chapter serves as your primer, breaking down the complex world of technology into digestible parts. We'll explore the different sectors within the tech industry, demystify key terminology, and identify the major players and trends shaping the future of tech.

Breaking Down Industry Sectors

The tech industry is vast and multifaceted. Understanding its various sectors will help you navigate this field with greater confidence:

- **Software Development**: This includes everything from application development to system software and enterprise solutions. Key areas to be familiar with include web development, mobile app development, and software engineering.

- **Hardware**: This sector involves physical technology products like computers, servers, and networking equipment. Understanding the basics of hardware design, manufacturing, and maintenance will give you insight into roles related to hardware engineering and IT infrastructure.

- **Cloud Computing**: Cloud services provide scalable computing resources over the internet. Key players like AWS, Microsoft Azure, and Google Cloud dominate this space. Familiarize yourself with cloud architecture, service models (IaaS, PaaS, SaaS), and cloud security.

- **Artificial Intelligence and Machine Learning**: AI and ML are revolutionizing many industries. Understand the fundamentals of these technologies, including natural language processing, neural networks, and data analytics. This knowledge will be crucial for recruiting roles related to data science and AI.

- **Cybersecurity**: With increasing digital threats, cybersecurity has become a critical area. Learn about common security practices, threat mitigation, and roles such as security analysts, ethical hackers, and compliance officers.

Basic Tech Terminology Made Simple

The tech industry has its own language. To communicate effectively with candidates and hiring managers, you'll need to grasp these essential terms:

- **Programming Languages**: Languages like Python, JavaScript, Java, and C++ are fundamental to software development. Each language has its own strengths and use cases.

- **Tech Stack**: A tech stack refers to the combination of technologies used to build and run an application. Common stacks include the MEAN stack (MongoDB, Express.js, Angular, Node.js) and the LAMP stack (Linux, Apache, MySQL, PHP).

- **APIs (Application Programming Interfaces)**: APIs allow different software systems to communicate with each other. Understanding how APIs work will help you assess candidates who work on integration and backend development.

- **DevOps**: DevOps is a set of practices that combines software development and IT operations to improve collaboration and efficiency. Key concepts include continuous integration/continuous deployment (CI/CD), automation, and containerization (e.g., Docker).

- **Agile and Scrum**: Agile is a project management methodology focused on iterative development and flexibility. Scrum is a framework within Agile that organizes work into sprints. Familiarity with these methodologies is essential for roles in project management and software development.

Key Players and Emerging Trends

To stay relevant in tech recruiting, you need to be aware of the major players and emerging trends in the industry:

- **Tech Giants**: Companies like Google, Apple, Microsoft, and Amazon are leaders in technology innovation. Understanding their product lines, corporate cultures, and hiring practices can provide insights into industry standards and expectations.

- **Startups and Scaleups**: The startup ecosystem is vibrant and dynamic. Keep an eye on emerging startups and scaleups in sectors like fintech, healthtech, and edtech. These companies often seek innovative tech talent to drive growth.

- **Trends to Watch**: Stay informed about trends such as the rise of remote work, advancements in AI and machine learning, and the growing focus on diversity and inclusion in tech. These trends will influence hiring practices and candidate expectations.

Conclusion: Laying the Groundwork

A comprehensive understanding of the tech industry is crucial for a successful transition into technical recruiting. By familiarizing yourself with different tech sectors, essential terminology, and industry trends, you'll be better equipped to engage with candidates and hiring managers alike. As we move forward, the next chapter will focus on building your tech fluency—transforming you from a general recruiter into a specialized technical recruiter.

In the next chapter, we'll dive into the practical steps of developing tech fluency, enabling you to speak the language of engineers with confidence and authority.

Chapter 3: Bridging the Gap – How to Build Tech Fluency

Subtitle: Learning to Speak the Language of Engineers

Introduction: The Power of Tech Fluency

To effectively recruit in the tech industry, you need more than just a basic understanding of technology—you need fluency. This chapter will guide you through the process of building tech fluency, transforming you from a generalist recruiter into a knowledgeable tech recruiter who can communicate effectively with engineers and technical teams.

Mastering the Tech Stack

Understanding the tech stack is fundamental to recruiting for technical roles. Here's how to get started:

- **Learn the Basics**: Begin with an overview of common tech stacks used in the industry. For example, the LAMP stack (Linux, Apache, MySQL, PHP) is popular for web development, while the MEAN stack (MongoDB, Express.js, Angular, Node.js) is often used for modern web applications. Knowing these will help you understand the technologies candidates are discussing.

- **Explore Full-Stack Development**: Full-stack developers work on both the front end (what users see) and the back end (server-side logic) of applications. Familiarize yourself with languages and frameworks used in both areas, such as HTML, CSS, JavaScript for the front end, and Node.js, Python, Ruby for the back end.

- **Understand Databases and Cloud Services**: Databases like SQL (MySQL, PostgreSQL) and NoSQL (MongoDB, Cassandra) store and manage data. Cloud services such as AWS, Azure, and Google Cloud offer scalable infrastructure. Knowing how these technologies work and their use cases will enhance your understanding of technical roles.

Self-Learning: Best Resources to Gain a Tech-Savvy Mindset

Building tech fluency involves continuous learning. Here are some resources and strategies to help you:

- **Online Courses and Certifications**: Platforms like Coursera, Udemy, and LinkedIn Learning offer courses on programming, cloud computing, and other tech topics. Consider taking courses to gain a deeper understanding of specific technologies or methodologies.

- **Tech Blogs and News Sites**: Follow tech blogs (e.g., TechCrunch, Ars Technica) and news sites to stay updated on industry trends and innovations. This will help you understand the context in which different technologies are used.

- **Tech Meetups and Webinars**: Attend local tech meetups, webinars, and industry conferences to network with tech professionals and learn about the latest advancements. Engaging with the tech community can provide valuable insights and practical knowledge.

- **Books and Documentation**: Read books and official documentation related to programming languages, frameworks, and technologies. Books such as *"Clean Code"* by Robert C. Martin and *"Design Patterns: Elements of Reusable Object-Oriented Software"* by Erich Gamma et al., can provide foundational knowledge.

Interviewing Engineers: How to Ask Questions that Matter

Effective interviewing is crucial for assessing technical talent. Here's how to approach it:

- **Prepare Technical Questions**: Develop questions that test candidates' understanding of key concepts and problem-solving skills. For example, you might ask about their experience with specific technologies, their approach to debugging, or how they would solve a particular technical problem.

- **Use Coding Challenges**: Incorporate coding challenges or technical assessments to evaluate candidates' practical skills. Tools like HackerRank or LeetCode can be used to administer coding tests and evaluate problem-solving abilities.

- **Understand the Role's Technical Requirements**: Tailor your questions to the specific technical requirements of the role. If a position requires expertise in a particular programming language or framework, focus your questions on those areas to gauge candidates' proficiency.

Communicating with Technical Teams

Effective communication with technical teams is key to successful recruiting:

- **Learn the Jargon**: Familiarize yourself with common technical terms and acronyms. While you don't need to be an expert, understanding terms like "API," "DevOps," and "microservices" will help you communicate more effectively.

- **Ask for Clarification**: Don't hesitate to ask technical team members for clarification on technical requirements or job descriptions. Understanding their needs and expectations will help you find better matches for their open positions.
- **Build Relationships**: Establish strong relationships with technical hiring managers and team members. Regularly check in with them to understand their evolving needs and preferences, and use their feedback to refine your recruiting strategies.

Conclusion: Becoming a Tech-Savvy Recruiter

Building tech fluency is a continuous process that requires dedication and curiosity. By mastering the tech stack, leveraging self-learning resources, developing effective interview techniques, and communicating well with technical teams, you'll enhance your ability to recruit top tech talent successfully.

In the next chapter, we'll focus on how to position yourself as a credible tech recruiter, transforming your newfound tech fluency into a powerful personal brand that attracts both candidates and clients.

Chapter 4: Reprogramming Your Pitch – Positioning Yourself as a Tech Recruiter

Subtitle: Branding Yourself in the Tech Recruiting Space

Introduction: Crafting a New Identity

Transitioning from a general recruiter to a technical recruiter is more than just acquiring knowledge—it's about rebranding yourself to stand out in a competitive field. In this chapter, we will explore how to reposition your personal brand to reflect your new tech expertise, optimize your online presence, and demonstrate your value to both candidates and hiring managers.

Updating Your Personal Brand: Crafting a Tech-Focused Resume

The first step in positioning yourself as a tech recruiter is refining your resume to showcase your technical recruiting capabilities. Here's how to make your resume stand out:

- **Highlight Tech Experience**: Emphasize any technical roles you've already filled, even if it was indirect or involved tech-adjacent roles. If you've recruited for engineering, IT, or product development positions, make that clear.

- **Showcase Your Knowledge**: Add certifications, courses, and self-learning initiatives that demonstrate your commitment to understanding technology. Listing relevant certifications like LinkedIn's Technical Recruiting course or Udemy's programming overviews can bolster your credibility.

- **Tailor Your Keywords**: Recruiters themselves get sourced by automated systems, so ensure your resume is optimized with keywords relevant to technical recruiting, such as "tech stack," "programming languages," "DevOps," and "software engineering."

- **Quantify Success**: Show the impact you've had in your previous recruiting roles. Metrics such as "reduced time-to-hire for technical positions by 30%" or "successfully placed over 50 engineers in high-demand roles" demonstrate your efficiency and capability in handling technical hires.

LinkedIn as Your Launchpad: Networking with Tech Professionals

Your LinkedIn profile is a critical tool in establishing your tech recruiter brand. Here's how to make the most of it:

- **Optimize Your Profile Headline**: Your headline should clearly state that you are a technical recruiter. Something like, "Technical Recruiter Specializing in Software Engineering, Data Science, and Cloud Computing" tells people exactly what you offer.

- **Revamp Your Summary**: Your summary should communicate your passion for technology and recruiting. Mention your tech fluency, any certifications, and your strategy for helping companies build strong technical teams.

- **Showcase Projects and Success Stories**: Use the "Featured" section to highlight key projects, blogs, or success stories in technical recruiting. Posting about recent tech hires, strategies for recruiting in a competitive market, or insights on emerging tech trends can solidify your expertise.

- **Engage with the Tech Community**: Join relevant LinkedIn groups (e.g., recruiting in tech, software engineering networks) and actively engage in discussions. Comment on posts, share tech-related articles, and publish your own content to attract a following among tech professionals and companies.

- **Connect with Tech Professionals**: Actively grow your network by connecting with engineers, developers, data scientists, and tech hiring managers. Follow key industry influencers and keep an eye on their insights and updates.

Showcasing Tech Insights in Your Professional Content

Creating and sharing content that reflects your expertise in tech recruiting is an excellent way to position yourself as a thought leader. Here are some content strategies:

- **Write Blog Posts**: Share your experiences and insights on tech recruiting. Topics could include "The Top Programming Languages in 2024" or "How to Evaluate Candidates for AI Roles." Posting on LinkedIn or a personal blog demonstrates your knowledge and thought leadership.

- **Curate Tech News**: Regularly share and comment on news related to the tech industry. Whether it's about the rise of AI or cloud adoption trends, curating timely, relevant content shows you're staying updated on tech developments.

- **Publish Case Studies**: If you've had success placing candidates in technical roles, write about those experiences. Highlight the challenges you faced, how you found the right candidates, and the results for the company. These case studies can act as powerful social proof of your expertise.

- **Engage in Webinars or Podcasts**: Participating in tech recruitment webinars or podcasts can further boost your credibility. Offering insights on recruiting strategies, challenges in hiring tech talent, or tech industry trends to a live audience is an effective way to position yourself as an expert.

Aligning with Tech Culture: Understanding What Matters to Tech Candidates

To stand out as a tech recruiter, you must understand the culture and values that matter to technical candidates. Here's what to keep in mind:

- **Work-Life Balance and Flexibility**: Many tech professionals prioritize flexible work hours, remote opportunities, and a healthy work-life balance. Being able to discuss these benefits can help you resonate with the candidates you're targeting.

- **Career Growth and Learning**: Tech candidates often value opportunities for learning new skills and career growth more than traditional perks. Knowing the potential career trajectories of tech roles can help you better position job offers and make them more appealing.

- **Company Culture Fit**: Engineers and developers often seek out companies with a strong, transparent culture. Understanding the cultural priorities of both the candidate and the company is key to finding good matches.

- **Cutting-Edge Technology**: Many tech professionals are attracted to companies that work on innovative projects or use the latest tools and frameworks. Highlighting these aspects of the role can make your pitch much more compelling.

Conclusion: Reprogramming Your Professional Identity

Positioning yourself as a technical recruiter involves more than just learning new skills—it's about rebranding and establishing your presence in the tech space. By crafting a tech-focused resume, optimizing your LinkedIn profile, sharing valuable content, and aligning with the needs of tech candidates, you'll stand out as a credible and trusted resource for both companies and candidates.

In the next chapter, we will dive into the tools and technologies that every successful technical recruiter must master to navigate this fast-paced world. You'll learn how to effectively leverage platforms like GitHub, Stack Overflow, and more to find top tech talent.

Chapter 5: The Recruiter's Toolkit – Mastering the Platforms and Tools of the Trade

Subtitle: Navigating GitHub, Stack Overflow, and Other Platforms to Find Top Talent

---

Introduction: Tools of the Technical Trade

Technical recruiting isn't just about finding candidates on traditional job boards. To thrive in the tech space, you need to dive deep into the platforms where developers, engineers, and tech professionals live and breathe their work. In this chapter, we'll explore the essential platforms and tools that will help you discover top talent, assess their skills, and streamline your recruiting process. From GitHub to Stack Overflow and beyond, we'll equip you with the digital toolkit you need to become a tech recruiting pro.

Understanding GitHub: The Portfolio of Developers

GitHub is more than just a code repository—it's a living portfolio where developers showcase their skills. Learning how to navigate GitHub can give you valuable insights into candidates' abilities, collaboration skills, and experience. Here's how to use it effectively:

- **Search for Candidates**: Use GitHub's search functionality to find developers based on specific programming languages, projects, or repositories. For example, you can search for "Python developers" or "JavaScript projects" to find candidates working in those languages.
- **Evaluate Repositories**: Look at candidates' repositories (repos) to assess their coding skills. A well-documented repo with clear structure, frequent updates, and collaborative work

(e.g., contributions to open-source projects) signals a strong developer.

- **Assess Engagement**: Pay attention to how often candidates contribute to projects, the number of "stars" and "forks" their repos have, and whether they collaborate with other developers. These metrics reflect their involvement and recognition in the developer community.

- **GitHub Profiles as Resumes**: A developer's GitHub profile can serve as a living resume. Check out their pinned projects, read their code, and explore their contributions to open-source projects. You'll gain a much clearer picture of their technical abilities than you would from a traditional resume alone.

Navigating Stack Overflow: Finding Problem-Solvers

Stack Overflow is where developers go to solve problems, exchange knowledge, and demonstrate their expertise. As a recruiter, it's an excellent resource for finding skilled candidates who are actively engaged in problem-solving. Here's how to leverage it:

- **Search by Tags**: Stack Overflow uses a tag system to categorize questions and answers by technology (e.g., JavaScript, Python, SQL). Use these tags to find developers with expertise in specific areas relevant to your open roles.

- **Review Contributions**: Look at the questions candidates have answered. Are their answers well-regarded by the community? A high "reputation" score indicates that they are knowledgeable and helpful. Top contributors often possess deep expertise in their chosen fields.

- **Engage with Candidates**: Stack Overflow allows users to contact developers directly if they have opted into being contacted for job opportunities. Personalize your messages by referencing their specific contributions or expertise, showing that you've taken the time to understand their skills.

- **Assess Problem-Solving Abilities**: Candidates who frequently answer questions on Stack Overflow are likely strong problem-solvers—a critical skill in technical roles. Their answers can give you a sense of their communication skills, technical knowledge, and approach to troubleshooting.

Leveraging LinkedIn for Tech Talent

While platforms like GitHub and Stack Overflow are essential for tech recruiting, LinkedIn remains a powerful tool for finding and connecting with candidates. Here's how to optimize LinkedIn for technical recruiting:

- **Use Boolean Searches**: Advanced Boolean searches can help you narrow down candidates with specific tech skills. For example, a search for "(Java OR Python) AND (DevOps OR Docker)" will return profiles of candidates with the relevant expertise.

- **Analyze Endorsements and Recommendations**: Look for candidates who have endorsements for tech skills from peers and colleagues. Recommendations from managers or fellow engineers can give you additional insights into their teamwork and communication skills.

- **LinkedIn Recruiter Tools**: If available, LinkedIn Recruiter offers advanced features like enhanced filters, access to more profiles, and InMail messaging. This tool can streamline your search process, making it easier to find candidates who match the technical qualifications you need.

- **Engage in LinkedIn Groups:** Join and actively participate in LinkedIn groups focused on software engineering, DevOps, AI, or other relevant tech topics. By sharing valuable insights or answering questions, you can position yourself as a knowledgeable recruiter, building credibility and attracting top-tier technical candidates organically.

- **Personalize Your Outreach:** When using InMail or connection requests, customize your messages based on each candidate's experience or interests. Reference their recent projects, blog posts, or open-source contributions to demonstrate that you've done your homework. Personalized messages lead to higher response rates and better engagement from passive candidates.

- **Showcase Tech Culture Through Posts:** Regularly share content on LinkedIn that highlights your company's tech culture—such as technical blog posts, behind-the-scenes videos of engineering teams, or case studies on recent projects. Highlighting innovative technologies or a strong developer community will attract top talent interested in those experiences and opportunities.

Mastering Technical Assessments and Coding Challenges

Assessing technical skills goes beyond reviewing resumes and profiles—you need to test candidates' abilities in a practical setting. Here's how to incorporate coding challenges and assessments into your recruitment process:

- **Platforms for Coding Tests**: Tools like HackerRank, Codility, and LeetCode allow you to create and send customized coding challenges to candidates. These platforms assess candidates' coding abilities, problem-solving skills, and even their approach to efficiency and optimization.

- **Tailor Assessments to Roles**: Make sure the coding challenges reflect the actual technical requirements of the position. For example, if you're hiring for a front-end developer role, focus on JavaScript and UI/UX problems, while a back-end role might emphasize databases, APIs, and server-side logic.

- **Time and Difficulty**: Be mindful of the time and difficulty level of the assessments. A challenge that is too long or difficult may frustrate candidates and deter top talent. On the other hand, a well-calibrated assessment will reveal a candidate's strengths and approach to problem-solving without overwhelming them.

- **Review Code Quality**: When reviewing results, pay attention not only to whether the candidate solved the problem, but also to how they wrote the code. Clean, well-organized, and efficient code is just as important as the final output.

Using Slack, Discord, and Other Developer Communities

Many developers are active in online communities outside of traditional recruiting platforms. Communities on Slack, Discord, Reddit, and other forums offer additional ways to engage with tech talent:

- **Join Developer Communities**: There are countless public Slack channels and Discord servers dedicated to specific programming languages, technologies, and frameworks. Joining these communities allows you to connect with developers in a more informal, natural setting.

- **Engage in Conversations**: Don't just lurk—actively participate in discussions. Asking thoughtful questions or sharing relevant articles can position you as a valuable member of the community and help you build relationships with potential candidates.

- **Network at Hackathons and Events**: Many online communities host hackathons, coding competitions, and virtual meetups. These events are a great opportunity to meet developers, see their work in action, and potentially recruit them for your open roles.

Conclusion: Building a Modern Recruiter's Toolkit

The key to success in technical recruiting lies in mastering the platforms and tools where tech talent lives. By familiarizing yourself with GitHub, Stack Overflow, LinkedIn, and technical assessment platforms, you'll be able to source, evaluate, and connect with top tech professionals more effectively.

In the next chapter, we'll explore the art of relationship-building in technical recruiting, showing you how to create lasting connections with candidates and foster long-term success in the competitive tech hiring market.

Chapter 6: Cultivating Connections – Building Relationships with Tech Talent

Subtitle: The Human Element Behind Technical Recruiting

Introduction: The Art of Relationship-Building

Technical recruiting isn't just about finding candidates with the right skillset—it's about building meaningful relationships that last beyond a single placement. The tech talent pool is highly competitive, and strong relationships can make all the difference in securing top candidates. In this chapter, we'll explore how to cultivate trust, communicate effectively, and nurture long-term connections that benefit both the candidate and your organization.

Understanding the Candidate's Journey: From Passive to Active

The tech talent landscape is unique in that many of the best candidates are often passive—they're not actively looking for a job but are open to the right opportunity. Here's how to approach both passive and active candidates:

- **Passive Candidates**: These candidates are currently employed and not actively applying for new roles. However, they may be open to hearing about exciting opportunities. To engage with passive candidates:
    - **Tailor Your Outreach**: Research their background thoroughly and craft personalized messages that highlight specific projects, technologies, or career growth opportunities relevant to them.
    - **Offer Value**: Instead of a hard sell, offer value by sharing industry insights, upcoming tech trends, or

networking opportunities. Position yourself as a helpful resource rather than just a recruiter looking to fill a role.

- **Active Candidates**: These candidates are already searching for new opportunities. When dealing with active candidates:

    - **Be Responsive**: Timely communication is key. Tech professionals, especially those with in-demand skills, receive multiple offers quickly. A slow response can mean losing top talent.

    - **Be Transparent**: Clearly outline the hiring process, timelines, and expectations. Active candidates appreciate transparency as it allows them to plan and compare other opportunities.

Building Trust in a Competitive Market

In the fast-paced world of tech recruiting, building trust is your most valuable currency. Candidates often rely on their recruiter for guidance, support, and industry insights. Here's how to cultivate trust:

- **Listen First, Sell Later**: During your initial conversations with candidates, focus on listening. Ask about their career goals, challenges, and what excites them about their work. Understanding their aspirations allows you to present opportunities that genuinely align with their ambitions.

- **Be Honest and Transparent**: If a role doesn't seem like a good fit, let the candidate know. Honesty will earn you long-term credibility, even if it means not filling a position right away. The candidate will appreciate your integrity and might consider you for future opportunities.

- **Follow Through on Promises**: Whether it's providing feedback after an interview or following up on a timeline, make sure you keep your word. Consistently delivering on your promises demonstrates reliability and professionalism.

- **Offer Career Advice**: Position yourself as a career advisor rather than just a recruiter. Candidates will appreciate any guidance you can provide, whether it's helping them improve their resume, preparing them for interviews, or advising on industry trends. Offering value in these ways strengthens the relationship.

Tailoring Your Communication Style for Tech Candidates

Tech candidates value efficiency, clarity, and technical details. The way you communicate plays a big role in how you build rapport with them. Here are a few strategies to adopt:

- **Get to the Point**: Avoid fluff and get straight to the details. Engineers and developers often prefer concise, direct communication that respects their time. For example, when discussing a job role, focus on the technologies, responsibilities, and impact rather than generic descriptions.

- **Understand Their Language**: Use the tech terminology you've learned. For instance, if you're recruiting for a cloud engineer, mention specific tools like AWS or Kubernetes. Demonstrating that you understand the technical aspects of the role boosts your credibility.

- **Respect Their Work Preferences**: Many tech professionals are introverted and prefer written communication (emails, messages) over calls. Adapt to their preferred communication style to ensure they feel comfortable during the recruiting process.

- **Offer Flexibility**: Tech talent often values flexibility in work schedules and remote opportunities. When discussing job roles, make sure to highlight any options for flexible hours or remote work. If flexibility isn't part of the role, be transparent about that upfront.

Nurturing Long-Term Relationships Beyond Placements

The relationship with a candidate doesn't end once they're placed in a role. Maintaining ongoing connections with your network is critical for future placements, referrals, and building your reputation. Here's how to nurture those relationships over time:

- **Follow-Up After Placement**: Check in with candidates a few weeks after they've started their new role. Ask how they're settling in, if the job is meeting their expectations, and if there's anything you can do to support them. This post-placement follow-up shows that you care about their long-term success.

- **Stay in Touch**: Keep the lines of communication open with your placed candidates and those you've previously interviewed. Share relevant industry news, job opportunities, or networking events with them periodically. This ongoing engagement can lead to referrals or even repeat placements when they're ready for the next career move.

- **Celebrate Milestones**: Recognize important milestones in your candidates' careers. Whether they've been promoted, received a certification, or worked on a notable project, acknowledging these achievements builds goodwill and strengthens your relationship.

- **Provide Ongoing Value**: Continue offering value even when a candidate isn't actively job-seeking. Whether it's sharing resources, providing career advice, or inviting them to industry events, showing that you're invested in their success keeps you top of mind.

Building a Referral Network

Tech professionals are often well-connected, and a strong referral network can be a powerful asset in your recruiting efforts. Here's how to leverage referrals:

- **Ask for Referrals Thoughtfully**: After building a solid relationship with a candidate or hire, don't hesitate to ask for referrals. A simple, "Do you know anyone else who might be a good fit for this role?" can yield great results.

- **Offer Incentives**: Many recruiters offer referral bonuses or incentives to candidates who refer top talent. This can be a great motivator, but be sure to pair it with a genuine interest in their network and connections.

- **Respect Their Network**: Always approach referrals with care. When someone refers a candidate, they are putting their own reputation on the line, so it's important to handle the process professionally and keep them informed about how the referral progresses.

Conclusion: Humanizing the Technical Recruiting Process

In a field driven by skill and data, the human element is often overlooked. Yet, building authentic relationships is the secret to long-term success in technical recruiting. By actively listening to your candidates, building trust through honesty and transparency, and nurturing ongoing relationships, you'll position yourself as a trusted partner in their career journey.

In the next chapter, we'll focus on how to collaborate effectively with hiring managers, ensuring that you not only understand the technical requirements of a role but also the team dynamics and company culture that drive successful hires.

Chapter 7: The Hiring Manager Partnership – Aligning Expectations and Delivering the Right Candidates

Subtitle: How to Build Trust, Manage Expectations, and Find the Perfect Fit

---

Introduction: The Power of the Recruiter-Hiring Manager Relationship

In technical recruiting, success hinges on more than just sourcing candidates with the right skills—it's about delivering the right candidates for the specific needs of the team. The hiring manager is your greatest ally in this mission. Developing a strong partnership with them can significantly improve your hiring process, ensuring you align expectations and make informed decisions. In this chapter, we'll explore how to build trust, communicate effectively, and set up the framework for delivering top talent that fits not only the role but also the company's culture and objectives.

Understanding the Hiring Manager's Needs

Before you can deliver the ideal candidate, you need to deeply understand what the hiring manager is looking for. This is often more than just a list of technical requirements—it's about the team dynamics, the company's goals, and the specific challenges the candidate will face on the job. Here's how to extract the key information you need:

- **Conduct a Discovery Meeting**: At the start of the hiring process, schedule a comprehensive meeting with the hiring manager to discuss their needs. This should go beyond reviewing the job description. Ask questions like:
    - What does success look like in this role?

- What are the top technical skills required?
- What kind of team culture does this candidate need to thrive in?
- Are there any upcoming projects or challenges that require specific expertise?

- **Clarify Must-Haves vs. Nice-to-Haves**: Hiring managers often provide a laundry list of skills, but not all are critical. Make sure to clarify which qualifications are absolutely necessary and which are flexible. This helps you narrow your search and avoid wasting time on candidates who don't meet the core criteria.

- **Understand Pain Points**: Ask about any past challenges in hiring for similar roles. Were there skills that previous candidates lacked? Were there difficulties with finding the right cultural fit? Understanding these pain points will guide you toward finding candidates who can succeed where others have struggled.

Managing Expectations: The Balancing Act

One of the most important (and delicate) aspects of your partnership with the hiring manager is managing expectations. It's common for managers to have an ideal candidate in mind—a "unicorn" who may not exist in the real world. Your role is to balance their expectations with the realities of the talent market. Here's how to manage this process diplomatically:

- **Set Realistic Timeframes**: Hiring managers often want the perfect candidate, and they want them fast. Be upfront about the time it might take to find a well-rounded technical candidate with the right skillset. If there's a need to move quickly, you may need to prioritize certain qualifications and compromise on others.

- **Educate About the Market**: Share data on the current tech talent market. For example, if there's a high demand for certain skill sets (e.g., cloud computing or machine learning), explain how that impacts availability and salary expectations. This helps hiring managers understand the competitive landscape and adjust their expectations accordingly.

- **Present a Range of Candidates**: Instead of focusing on finding one perfect candidate, present a range of options. This allows the hiring manager to compare and contrast candidates with different strengths. For instance, one candidate might have strong technical skills but less experience, while another may have a broader range of skills but higher salary requirements.

- **Stay Flexible and Iterative**: Recruiting is not always a linear process. Sometimes, you'll need to iterate based on feedback. If a candidate doesn't quite fit, ask the hiring manager what they liked and didn't like about that person. Use this feedback to refine your search, keeping the lines of communication open.

Crafting a Collaborative Hiring Strategy

The most successful technical recruiters work hand-in-hand with hiring managers to craft a collaborative hiring strategy. This ensures that both parties are aligned from the start and can avoid unnecessary delays or miscommunications. Here's how to create a winning strategy:

- **Define Clear Milestones**: Set measurable goals and checkpoints throughout the hiring process. This could include timelines for sourcing, candidate review, and interviews.

Agreeing on these milestones ensures that both you and the hiring manager are on the same page regarding timelines and expectations.

- **Involve the Team**: Hiring managers often consult with their team during the interview process, especially for technical roles that require input from peers or senior engineers. Make sure you understand how the team will be involved and factor in time for peer interviews or technical assessments.

- **Customize the Interview Process**: Work with the hiring manager to design an interview process that assesses both technical skills and cultural fit. For example, coding challenges or whiteboard sessions can evaluate problem-solving abilities, while behavioral interviews help gauge how the candidate will integrate with the team. The hiring manager's input is crucial to tailoring this process to the specific role.

Navigating the Interview Process Together

Once you've sourced candidates, the next step is to work closely with the hiring manager throughout the interview process. This collaboration is essential to ensure the process runs smoothly and efficiently:

- **Pre-Interview Prep**: Make sure both you and the hiring manager are aligned on how the interview will be structured. Share the candidate's resume, LinkedIn profile, and any notes about their background. If the candidate completed a technical assessment, review the results together to highlight key areas for follow-up.

- **Interview Feedback**: After each interview, gather feedback promptly. Establish a feedback loop where both you and the hiring manager discuss the candidate's performance. Was the candidate's technical ability up to par? Did they seem like a good cultural fit? Timely and structured feedback is key to keeping the process moving.

- **Handle Objections and Concerns**: Sometimes, hiring managers have concerns about a candidate after an interview. Address these concerns head-on, providing additional context or suggesting ways the candidate could still meet the requirements with some additional support or training.

The Hiring Decision: Data-Driven and Collaborative

The final decision to hire a candidate should always be a collaborative effort between the recruiter and the hiring manager. It's important to ensure that the decision is based on both data and insights from the interview process:

- **Review Data Together**: Use any available data to support your decision. This could include coding challenge scores, technical assessment results, or feedback from team members who interviewed the candidate. Present a holistic view of each candidate's strengths and areas for improvement.

- **Balance Skills and Culture Fit**: Hiring managers often focus heavily on technical skills, but cultural fit is equally important. If a candidate has slightly less experience but fits in well with the team culture, don't be afraid to advocate for them. It's easier to train technical skills than to change someone's attitude or work style.

- **Make Informed Trade-Offs**: In some cases, you won't find a candidate who checks every single box. Work with the hiring manager to make informed trade-offs, whether it's prioritizing attitude and culture fit over technical experience or choosing someone who may require a higher salary but brings long-term value.

Communicating the Offer: Closing with Confidence

Once you've identified the right candidate, closing the deal requires seamless communication between you and the hiring manager. Here's how to collaborate on the final steps:

- **Align on the Offer Package**: Make sure the hiring manager is involved in crafting the offer. Consider the candidate's salary expectations, benefits, remote work options, and other factors that could influence their decision. A competitive offer reflects the value the candidate will bring to the organization.

- **Personalized Offer Delivery**: Work together to deliver the offer in a personalized way. The hiring manager's involvement in extending the offer can show the candidate how invested the company is in their success. A personal touch can make a big difference, especially when closing in a competitive market.

- **Manage Counteroffers**: Candidates in tech often receive counteroffers from their current employer or other companies. Prepare the hiring manager for the possibility of a counteroffer, and discuss strategies to address it proactively. Flexibility in the offer package or career growth opportunities can help seal the deal.

Conclusion: Building a Strong Partnership for Long-Term Success

A strong partnership with the hiring manager is the backbone of successful technical recruiting. By understanding their needs, managing expectations, collaborating on strategy, and navigating the interview process together, you'll create a seamless experience that results in better hires and a more efficient recruiting process.

In the next chapter, we'll focus on the final phase of the process—onboarding technical talent and setting them up for success within their new role, ensuring they hit the ground running from day one.

Chapter 8: Seamless Onboarding – Setting Technical Talent Up for Success

Subtitle: From Offer Acceptance to Full Integration, How to Ensure a Smooth Transition

---

Introduction: The Critical First Steps After the Hire

Your job doesn't end when the offer is accepted. In fact, the onboarding process is where successful hiring is truly solidified. A well-structured onboarding experience can mean the difference between a technical hire thriving or struggling in their new role. In this chapter, we'll cover everything you need to know to ensure a smooth transition from offer acceptance to full integration into the company. You'll learn how to collaborate with HR, support hiring managers, and make the onboarding process a pivotal part of your recruitment strategy.

Why Onboarding Matters More Than You Think

Technical talent, especially in-demand developers and engineers, often have multiple job offers on the table. First impressions after hiring can significantly impact how they perceive the company, their role, and their future within the organization. Here's why effective onboarding matters:

- **Reducing Turnover**: Studies show that strong onboarding processes improve employee retention. When tech hires feel welcomed, supported, and set up for success from day one, they're more likely to stay long-term.
- **Accelerating Productivity**: Proper onboarding ensures that new hires quickly acclimate to the team and their tasks. This

minimizes the downtime as they learn company processes, systems, and tools, allowing them to contribute faster.

- **Building Loyalty and Engagement**: A positive onboarding experience makes new employees feel valued. They'll feel connected to the company's mission and more engaged in their work, which directly impacts performance and innovation.

The Pre-Boarding Process: Setting Expectations Early

Onboarding begins before the employee's first day. The pre-boarding process is an essential step to ensure a smooth transition. Here's how to get started:

- **Send a Welcome Package**: Before their start date, send a welcome package to the new hire. This can include company swag, a personalized welcome letter, and any necessary paperwork or login details for company systems. A well-prepared package creates a positive first impression and builds excitement.

- **Prepare the Tools and Resources**: Make sure that the new hire has access to all necessary hardware, software, and tools on day one. This includes setting up company email accounts, Slack or Microsoft Teams access, and any development environments or tech stacks they'll need.

- **Outline the First Week Schedule**: Send a detailed schedule for the first week, outlining training sessions, team introductions, and any onboarding meetings. Having a clear roadmap helps new employees feel more confident and less anxious about their first days.

Collaborating with HR for a Smooth Transition

Your role as a recruiter doesn't stop once the candidate accepts the offer. Collaborating closely with HR ensures that all administrative and legal aspects of onboarding are handled efficiently, so the new hire can focus on their role. Here's how to ensure a smooth handoff:

- **Communicate the Candidate's Needs**: If the candidate has specific requests (such as flexible work hours, relocation assistance, or visa support), make sure HR is aware of these details early. Addressing these needs in advance ensures that there are no surprises or delays during the onboarding process.

- **Ensure Compliance**: Every company has compliance-related steps in the onboarding process, from signing contracts to completing tax forms. Stay in touch with HR to ensure all paperwork is completed and any legal requirements are met before the candidate's start date.

- **Coordinate Onboarding Meetings**: Work with HR to set up any mandatory onboarding meetings, such as orientation sessions, benefits presentations, or company policy overviews. This allows you to focus on the more role-specific elements of onboarding, while HR handles the administrative side.

Day One: Making a Strong First Impression

The first day sets the tone for the new hire's experience with the company. Ensuring that everything runs smoothly on day one is crucial for making a positive impression. Here's how to do it right:

- **Welcome in Person (or Virtually)**: Whether your company operates in person or remotely, make sure someone is available to greet the new hire personally. If remote, schedule a video call to introduce them to the team. This personal touch makes the new employee feel welcomed and valued right from the start.

- **Facilitate a Team Introduction**: Arrange a team meeting, either in person or via video chat, so the new hire can meet their colleagues. Provide context for the introductions by explaining how their role fits into the team structure and what everyone else's roles are.

- **Tour the Office or Virtual Workspace**: If working in person, give the new hire a tour of the office, including key areas like the break room, restrooms, and important meeting spaces. If they're working remotely, offer a "virtual tour" of the tools and platforms they'll be using, such as project management software or communication tools.

Chapter 9: Measuring Success – Tracking Key Metrics and Demonstrating Your Value

Subtitle: Using Data to Improve Your Technical Recruiting Strategy and Prove Your Impact

---

Introduction: The Data-Driven Recruiter

In today's competitive job market, success as a Technical Recruiter isn't just about filling positions; it's about doing so efficiently and effectively. To achieve this, you need to measure your performance using data and key metrics. Tracking the right metrics helps you optimize your processes, demonstrate your value to stakeholders, and continually improve your recruiting strategy. In this chapter, we'll explore how to track essential recruitment metrics, use data to inform decision-making, and effectively communicate your impact to hiring managers and leadership.

Why Metrics Matter in Technical Recruiting

Recruiting for technical roles is often complex, with longer time-to-hire, high-demand skillsets, and intense competition for top candidates. Metrics allow you to:

- **Identify Bottlenecks**: Tracking your recruitment process helps you pinpoint inefficiencies or areas that need improvement, such as long interview times or low offer acceptance rates.

- **Improve Candidate Experience**: Data on candidate experience, from initial contact to offer, can highlight areas where you can improve communication or streamline the process.

- **Demonstrate ROI**: By showing the time and cost savings of your recruiting efforts, you prove your value to the company and secure buy-in from leadership for new tools, resources, or team expansion.

Key Metrics to Track in Technical Recruiting

Here are some of the most critical metrics you should be tracking to measure your performance and identify opportunities for improvement:

1. Time-to-Fill and Time-to-Hire

- **Time-to-Fill**: This metric measures the number of days between the job being posted and when a candidate accepts the offer. It's a good indicator of how efficient your recruiting process is, from sourcing to offer acceptance.
- **Time-to-Hire**: This tracks the time between when a candidate is first contacted and when they accept the offer. It's a more candidate-focused metric and can help you assess how quickly you can engage and close top technical talent.

Why It Matters: A long time-to-fill or time-to-hire can mean lost opportunities, especially in technical recruiting, where in-demand candidates are likely receiving multiple offers. Keeping these metrics low ensures you're moving quickly and staying competitive.

How to Improve It: If your time-to-fill or time-to-hire is high, examine potential bottlenecks. Are interviews taking too long to schedule? Are hiring managers taking too long to give feedback? Streamlining communication and decision-making can reduce this timeline.

2. Quality of Hire

- **Definition**: Quality of hire measures the performance of the new hires once they're in their role. This could be based on performance reviews, productivity metrics, or feedback from managers.

Why It Matters: Quality of hire is one of the best indicators of recruiting success. Hiring quickly is important, but hiring the *right* person for the job is what ultimately drives value for the organization.

How to Improve It: To improve this metric, focus on aligning more closely with hiring managers, ensuring the job description is accurate, and using behavioral interview techniques to assess cultural fit. Gathering feedback from managers about recent hires can help refine your process.

---

3. Source of Hire

- **Definition**: This metric tracks where your hires are coming from—whether it's job boards, LinkedIn, referrals, or agency partnerships.

Why It Matters: Understanding your most effective sourcing channels allows you to focus your efforts and budget on what works best. For example, if referrals tend to result in higher-quality hires, you may want to invest more in employee referral programs.

How to Improve It: Track the performance of different channels over time. If one channel consistently provides low-quality candidates, it may be time to reevaluate its use or experiment with new sourcing methods like specialized technical communities or coding bootcamps.

---

4. Offer Acceptance Rate

- **Definition**: This metric tracks the percentage of offers extended to candidates that are accepted.

Why It Matters: A low offer acceptance rate could signal that candidates are receiving more competitive offers from other companies, or that there's a disconnect between the candidate's expectations and the offer package.

How to Improve It: If your offer acceptance rate is low, work with hiring managers to ensure the offer is competitive. Stay informed about market salary rates, and be ready to negotiate. Also, maintain open communication with candidates throughout the process to gauge their interest and address any concerns early.

5. Candidate Experience and Net Promoter Score (NPS)

- **Definition**: Candidate NPS is a measure of how likely candidates are to recommend your company's recruiting process to others. This metric is based on candidate surveys and feedback after the recruiting process, whether they were hired or not.

Why It Matters: A positive candidate experience is essential for maintaining your company's reputation in a highly competitive technical market. Even candidates who weren't hired can become advocates for your company if they had a good experience.

How to Improve It: To boost this metric, focus on clear and timely communication with candidates. Offer constructive feedback to those who didn't get the role, and ensure a positive experience at every stage of the process, from initial outreach to offer negotiation.

6. Diversity Hiring Metrics

- **Definition**: These metrics track how well you're sourcing and hiring candidates from underrepresented groups, such as women, people of color, or individuals from non-traditional educational backgrounds.

Why It Matters: Diverse teams drive innovation, and many companies are prioritizing diversity hiring as a core strategy. Tracking your progress ensures you're making headway in creating an inclusive environment.

How to Improve It: To improve diversity metrics, expand your sourcing efforts to include more diverse talent pools. Partner with coding bootcamps or organizations that focus on underrepresented groups in tech, and be mindful of potential biases in your hiring process.

Using Data to Inform Your Recruiting Strategy

Collecting data is just the first step. The real power comes from analyzing that data and using it to inform your recruiting strategy. Here's how to leverage your data effectively:

- **Analyze Trends Over Time**: Don't just look at your metrics in isolation. Track them over time to identify trends. For example, is your time-to-fill increasing or decreasing? Are you consistently seeing high-quality candidates from certain sources? Use these insights to adjust your approach.

- **Benchmark Against Industry Standards**: Compare your metrics to industry benchmarks to see how you stack up. Are you filling roles faster than the average in your industry? Are your offer acceptance rates in line with competitors? Understanding your position in the market helps you stay competitive.

- **A/B Test New Strategies**: If a particular sourcing channel isn't delivering results, don't be afraid to experiment with new strategies. A/B testing different approaches—such as reaching out to candidates with different messaging or trying new job boards—can help you fine-tune your process.

Communicating Your Impact to Stakeholders

It's not enough to track metrics internally. You need to communicate your recruiting success to stakeholders—hiring managers, HR, and leadership—to demonstrate your value and secure buy-in for future initiatives. Here's how to do it:

- **Present Regular Reports**: Create clear, data-driven reports that highlight your key metrics and performance. Include visuals like charts or graphs to make the data easier to digest. Present these reports regularly—monthly or quarterly—so stakeholders are always aware of your contributions.

- **Tell the Story Behind the Numbers**: Numbers are important, but the context is key. Explain why your time-to-fill might be longer for certain technical roles due to the complexity of the skills required. Show how improving your sourcing strategy led to higher-quality hires or shorter hiring times.

- **Highlight Wins and Areas for Growth**: Share your successes, but also be transparent about areas where you can improve. This builds trust with stakeholders and shows that you're constantly looking to refine and optimize your process.

Conclusion: Proving Your Value as a Data-Driven Recruiter

Being a successful Technical Recruiter means more than just finding candidates—it's about measuring your performance, optimizing your strategy, and demonstrating your value to the organization. By tracking the right metrics and using data to inform your decisions, you not only improve your own efficiency but also prove your impact on the company's growth and success.

In the final chapter, we'll wrap up the journey from recruiter to Technical Recruiter, exploring the ongoing learning and evolution required to stay at the top of your game in the ever-changing world of tech talent acquisition.

Chapter 10: The Future of Technical Recruiting – Staying Ahead in an Evolving Landscape

Subtitle: Continuous Learning, Emerging Trends, and Shaping the Future of Your Career

---

Introduction: Why Technical Recruiting Never Stays the Same

The field of technical recruiting is dynamic, constantly shaped by advances in technology, shifts in the talent market, and evolving expectations from both candidates and companies. To stay ahead and continue growing in your role, you must embrace continuous learning and be ready to adapt to new trends. In this final chapter, we'll explore the key skills and knowledge areas you need to future-proof your career in technical recruiting, dive into emerging trends shaping the industry, and outline how you can become a thought leader in this space.

The Importance of Lifelong Learning in Technical Recruiting

Technical recruiting is one of the few fields where constant learning is not just encouraged but required. The technologies that developers and engineers use are continually evolving, and staying up-to-date with them is essential if you want to remain relevant in your role.

Here's how to keep learning as part of your professional development:

- **Follow Industry News and Trends**: Make it a habit to read tech blogs, follow industry news, and subscribe to recruiting newsletters. Stay informed about shifts in the job market, changes in popular programming languages, and emerging tech tools that your candidates will likely be using.

- **Take Technical Courses**: You don't need to become a coder, but understanding the basics of coding languages, development environments, and tech trends will help you speak the language of your candidates. Online platforms like Coursera, Udemy, and edX offer introductory courses in various technical topics, from Python to AI to cloud computing.
- **Join Professional Networks and Communities**: Networking is a powerful tool for continuous learning. Join recruiter groups on LinkedIn, attend industry conferences, or participate in tech meetups. Engaging with other recruiters and tech professionals can provide insights, share best practices, and help you stay ahead of the curve.

Key Emerging Trends in Technical Recruiting

To remain competitive and effective, technical recruiters need to be aware of the following emerging trends that are likely to shape the future of talent acquisition:

1. Artificial Intelligence and Automation in Recruitment

AI-powered tools are transforming the recruitment process, from sourcing candidates to conducting initial screening interviews. Here's how you can leverage AI to improve your efficiency:

- **Automated Candidate Screening**: AI tools can analyze resumes and profiles to identify the best-fit candidates based on predefined criteria. This can significantly reduce the time spent on initial screening.
- **Chatbots for Candidate Engagement**: Chatbots can handle routine questions from candidates, provide information about

open roles, and even schedule interviews, freeing up more of your time for high-value tasks.

- **AI for Diversity and Inclusion**: AI tools are being developed to reduce bias in recruiting by anonymizing candidate profiles and using data-driven assessments to ensure that every candidate is evaluated based on merit rather than unconscious biases.

Action Plan: As AI tools continue to develop, make sure you stay informed about new technologies that can enhance your recruiting process. Learn how to integrate these tools into your workflow while ensuring that human oversight remains to maintain fairness and accuracy.

2. The Rise of Remote Work and Global Talent Pools

The COVID-19 pandemic accelerated the shift toward remote work, and many companies now offer fully remote or hybrid roles. This shift has expanded the talent pool beyond geographical limitations, allowing companies to hire talent from anywhere in the world.

- **Sourcing Global Talent**: You'll need to develop strategies to source candidates from diverse geographical locations. This includes becoming familiar with different job boards, recruitment platforms, and online communities that are popular in various regions.
- **Navigating Global Hiring Challenges**: With global talent comes complexity. Understand local labor laws, cultural nuances, and time zone challenges when recruiting internationally. Partner with legal and HR teams to ensure smooth onboarding for global hires.

- **Employer Branding for Remote Work**: Companies must now compete not just on salary or office perks, but on their remote work culture. Help your clients or company build a strong employer brand that emphasizes flexibility, work-life balance, and opportunities for remote employees.

Action Plan: Become an expert in remote recruitment. Familiarize yourself with international hiring processes, time zone management, and remote onboarding strategies. Stay up to date on how remote work is influencing the future of work.

---

3. The Shift Toward Skills-Based Hiring

More companies are moving away from traditional degree requirements in favor of skills-based hiring. This trend is particularly relevant in technical roles, where many top engineers and developers are self-taught or have non-traditional educational backgrounds.

- **Evaluating Skills Over Credentials**: Learn to assess a candidate's technical skills through coding challenges, portfolio reviews, and technical interviews, rather than relying solely on resumes or educational background.

- **Leveraging Alternative Talent Sources**: Bootcamps, online learning platforms, and coding competitions are excellent sources of tech talent. These candidates may not have formal degrees but possess the necessary skills to succeed in technical roles.

- **Implementing Skills Assessments**: Collaborate with hiring managers to implement skills-based assessments as part of the hiring process. This might include coding tests, problem-solving exercises, or even real-world technical projects.

Action Plan: Work closely with hiring managers to prioritize skills-based hiring. Learn how to evaluate technical competencies and build relationships with alternative talent sources like bootcamps, hackathons, and coding communities.

---

4. Diversity, Equity, and Inclusion (DEI) as a Recruiting Priority

Diversity and inclusion initiatives are at the forefront of talent acquisition strategies today. The Top Companies recognize that diverse teams are more innovative, creative, and successful overall. Here's how you can contribute to your company's DEI goals:

- **Sourcing from Diverse Talent Pools**: Be proactive in sourcing candidates from underrepresented qualified groups by attending diversity-focused job fairs, engaging with ERGs (Employee Resource Groups), and reaching out to organizations that support marginalized talent in tech.

- **Reducing Bias in Hiring**: Use structured interviews, standardized evaluations, and AI tools that help reduce unconscious bias in the hiring process. Ensure that you and the hiring team are trained on bias awareness and inclusive hiring practices.

- **Championing an Inclusive Culture**: Beyond hiring, help ensure that new employees from diverse backgrounds feel supported and included. Partner with HR to ensure that onboarding programs emphasize diversity and foster an inclusive company culture.

Action Plan: Today's politics aside, make DEI a priority in your recruiting strategy. Collaborate with HR, implement diverse sourcing strategies, and advocate for inclusivity throughout the hiring process.

Becoming a Thought Leader in Technical Recruiting

The most successful recruiters don't just follow trends—they set them. As you evolve in your role, you can position yourself as a thought leader in the technical recruiting space. Here's how:

- **Share Your Knowledge**: Write articles, create LinkedIn posts, or start a blog where you share insights about the industry, emerging trends, or best practices in technical recruiting. This not only helps others but also builds your personal brand.

- **Engage in Speaking Opportunities**: Look for opportunities to speak at industry conferences, webinars, or podcasts. Sharing your expertise with others not only solidifies your reputation but also keeps you connected with the latest developments in the field.

- **Mentor New Recruiters**: As you gain more experience, offer to mentor newer recruiters looking to break into technical recruiting. Helping others succeed elevates your leadership profile and expands your network.

Action Plan: Start by creating a content calendar for thought leadership. Whether it's writing a blog, recording videos, or engaging in public speaking, actively contribute to the professional conversation around technical recruiting.

Conclusion: The Journey Ahead – Shaping Your Future in Technical Recruiting

Your transition from recruiter to technical recruiter is only the beginning of a long and fulfilling career in one of the most dynamic and impactful roles in the talent acquisition space. By staying curious, continuously learning, and adapting to the ever-changing world of technology and talent, you'll position yourself not just as a recruiter but as a strategic partner to the companies and candidates you serve.

Remember, technical recruiting isn't just about filling positions—it's about shaping the future of teams, products, and industries. And as the landscape continues to evolve, you're ready to grow alongside it.

Thank you for embarking on this journey. Now go out and recruit the future!

Final Thoughts: What's Next?

Congratulations!!! - You've just completed my book on making the transition to Technical Recruiter! The next step is putting these solid strategies into action. Whether you're preparing for your first technical recruiter role or seeking to refine your skills, remember that technical recruiting is a journey of continuous improvement.

Keep learning, stay connected to industry trends, and embrace the challenges ahead. The future of technical recruiting is bright—and you're now prepared to be at the forefront of it.

All the Best!!!!

Jon D. McClain

Recommended Resources and Tools for Tech Recruiting

1. Sourcing Platforms & Tools

- **LinkedIn Recruiter**: Essential for sourcing and engaging passive tech talent. Use Boolean search techniques to find niche skillsets.

- **GitHub**: Great for assessing technical skills through code repositories. Look for activity on projects, contributions to open-source work, and collaboration history.

- **Stack Overflow**: Identify top problem-solvers and developers by reviewing answers to tech questions and checking reputation scores.

- **HackerRank & Codility**: Use these platforms for coding challenges and technical assessments to evaluate candidates' practical skills before interviews.

- **AngelList**: Ideal for finding startup talent and candidates who thrive in entrepreneurial environments.

2. Tech-Specific Job Boards

- **Hired**: A marketplace that connects vetted tech candidates directly with hiring companies. Great for software engineers, product managers, and UX/UI designers.

- **Dice**: Specializes in tech jobs, offering a deep candidate pool for roles like developers, system administrators, and data scientists.

- **BuiltIn**: This platform features job postings for tech companies, particularly startups, in major cities across the US.

- **Stack Overflow Jobs**: In addition to the Q&A platform, Stack Overflow has a dedicated job board for tech professionals.

3. Boolean Search Tips

- **LinkedIn Boolean Search**: Use specific strings like ("Python" OR "Java") AND "AWS" AND ("Full-Stack" OR "DevOps") to narrow down your search to the exact skillset.

- **Google X-Ray Search**: Use site:github.com "Python developer" location: "Seattle" to source developers from GitHub based on location and expertise.

- **Social Media Search**: Utilize Twitter's advanced search to find developers discussing specific technologies by tracking hashtags like #javascript, #datascience.

4. Tech Communities & Networks

- **Slack & Discord Communities**: Join tech-focused groups where developers actively discuss technologies, challenges, and innovations. Examples: "Techqueria" (for Latinx professionals in tech), "Women Who Code".

- **Meetup.com**: Find local and virtual meetups related to specific tech stacks (e.g., DevOps, AI, Full-Stack Development).

- **Reddit**: Subreddits like r/cscareerquestions or r/programming can be good sources for understanding tech talent and their concerns.

5. Learning Resources for Staying Updated

- **Coursera/Udemy/edX**: Stay updated on tech trends and foundational knowledge (courses on AI, cloud computing, etc.) to better understand the roles you're recruiting for.

- **TechCrunch/Ars Technica**: Follow these news sources to stay up-to-date with industry trends, acquisitions, and market shifts.

- **O'Reilly Media**: A treasure trove of technical books and online courses covering the latest in software development, machine learning, and more.

Glossary of Technical Terms for Tech Recruiters

Acceleration
In Software Engineering, Acceleration refers to the increase in the speed of processing, performance, or execution of a System or Application. It often involves optimizing code, utilizing hardware improvements, or applying specialized techniques like parallel processing, caching, or hardware accelerators (e.g., GPUs) to reduce latency and enhance efficiency in software operations.

Algorithm
A step-by-step procedure or formula for solving a problem. In programming, algorithms are used to manipulate data, perform calculations, or automate tasks. Understanding basic algorithms is crucial when evaluating a candidate's problem-solving abilities.

Automation
In software engineering, automation refers to the use of technology and tools to perform tasks with minimal human intervention. It is commonly applied in areas such as testing (e.g., automated testing with tools like Selenium, Cypress), deployment (e.g., continuous integration/continuous delivery (CI/CD) pipelines using Jenkins, GitLab CI), and infrastructure management (e.g., Infrastructure as Code (IaC) with tools like Terraform or Ansible). Automation increases efficiency, reduces errors, and accelerates development cycles by streamlining repetitive or complex processes.

AWS (Amazon Web Services)
A comprehensive cloud computing platform provided by Amazon.

AWS offers services like computing power (EC2), storage (S3), and databases (RDS). AWS certifications and experience are highly valued for cloud-related roles

Big Data
Refers to extremely large datasets that are analyzed computationally to reveal patterns, trends, and associations, especially relating to human behavior and interactions. Big data technologies include Hadoop, Apache Spark, and NoSQL databases.

C++
A high-performance, object-oriented programming language commonly used in system/software development, game development, and applications requiring real-time processing, like high-frequency trading.

CI/CD (Continuous Integration/Continuous Deployment)
A method used in DevOps practices to automate the process of integrating code changes (CI) and deploying them to production environments (CD). It ensures rapid and reliable software updates. Tools like Jenkins, TravisCI, and CircleCI are used to implement CI/CD pipelines.

Cloud Systems
Technology infrastructures that provide computing services over the internet, including servers, storage, and applications. Common cloud platforms include AWS, Google Cloud, and Microsoft Azure. Cloud expertise is highly sought after for DevOps and infrastructure roles.

Coding Interview Prep
The process tech candidates go through to prepare for interviews,

often involving coding challenges, algorithms, and problem-solving exercises. Platforms like LeetCode, HackerRank, and CodeSignal are popular for interview preparation.

DevOps
A set of practices that combines software development (Dev) and IT operations (Ops), aiming to shorten the development lifecycle and provide continuous delivery of high-quality software. Tools include Jenkins, Docker, and Kubernetes.

Engineering Productivity
At Google, *Engineering Productivity* refers to the practice of improving developer efficiency and effectiveness through tools, processes, and infrastructure optimizations. It involves creating systems that reduce the time engineers spend on repetitive tasks, testing, and deployment, allowing them to focus on innovation and code quality. This is often achieved through advanced CI/CD pipelines, automated testing frameworks, code review tools, and infrastructure management. Teams dedicated to Engineering Productivity (often called Developer Productivity or DevEx at other companies) focus on streamlining workflows, reducing bottlenecks, and enhancing collaboration across engineering teams, ultimately accelerating product development cycles.

(M)FAANG
An updated acronym representing the major tech companies: **Microsoft**, **Facebook**, **Apple**, **Amazon**, **Netflix**, and **Google**. These companies are known for offering competitive compensation, challenging interview processes, and opportunities to work on cutting-edge technology.

Frameworks

Pre-built software structures that provide a foundation for developing applications. Popular web development frameworks include **React**, **Angular**, **Vue.js** (front-end), and **Django**, **Flask**, **Spring** (back-end). Frameworks simplify the development process by offering reusable code and modular components.

Java

Java is a versatile, object-oriented programming language widely used for building large-scale enterprise applications, web applications, and Android mobile apps. Known for its platform independence via the Java Virtual Machine (JVM), it allows developers to write code once and run it anywhere. Java is commonly used in backend development with frameworks like Spring and Hibernate, and in microservices architectures. Its robustness, extensive libraries, and strong community support make it a popular choice for scalable, high-performance systems.

JavaScript

A dynamic programming language commonly used in web development to create interactive elements on websites. JavaScript frameworks and libraries like React, Angular, and Vue.js are popular for building user interfaces.

Machine Learning (ML)

A subset of artificial intelligence (AI) that allows systems to automatically learn from data and improve from experience without being explicitly programmed. Common frameworks include TensorFlow, PyTorch, and Scikit-learn.

Python

A high-level, interpreted programming language known for its simplicity and readability. It's widely used in web development, data science, machine learning, and automation. Python is a preferred language for data analysis and AI applications.

Scalability

The ability of a system, application, or infrastructure to handle increased load—such as more users, data, or traffic—without compromising performance or reliability. Scalable systems are designed to grow efficiently by adding resources like servers, memory, or processing power, either vertically (upgrading existing machines) or horizontally (adding more machines). Scalability is a key concern in designing backend systems, cloud services, and distributed applications, ensuring they can support growth and high availability over time.

Scripting

Writing short programs or scripts to automate tasks or manipulate data. Scripting languages like Python, Ruby, and Bash are commonly used for automation in system administration, data processing, and testing.

Testing

The process of verifying that software functions as expected. Various testing methods include unit testing (testing individual components), integration testing (testing how components work together), and automated testing (using tools like Selenium, JUnit, or pytest to run tests automatically).

The Ultimate Job Hunter's Toolkit for Aspiring Technical Recruiters
Your Go-To Guide for Job Boards, Networking Communities, Certifications, and Career Opportunities in Tech Recruiting

---

Job Search Platforms

1. **LinkedIn Jobs** – The go-to platform for professional networking and job searching, offering numerous technical recruiter roles and networking opportunities.
    - LinkedIn Jobs
    - https://www.linkedin.com/jobs/
2. **Indeed** – A major job board with a wide array of recruiter positions, including technical recruiting roles.
    - Indeed
    - https://www.indeed.com/
3. **Glassdoor** – Offers job listings along with reviews from current and past employees, giving insights into company culture.
    - Glassdoor
    - https://www.glassdoor.com/
4. **ZipRecruiter** – A platform with recruiter jobs across various industries, including tech recruiting.
    - ZipRecruiter
    - https://www.ziprecruiter.com/
5. **AngelList** – Specialized in startup roles, this is a great resource for finding tech recruiter jobs in growing tech companies.
    - AngelList

- https://angel.co/jobs
6. **Hired** – A job marketplace focused on tech jobs, allowing technical recruiters to connect with top tech companies.
    - Hired
    - https://hired.com/
7. **BuiltIn** – Features job postings for technical recruiters in startup and tech-heavy environments, with a focus on major tech hubs.
    - BuiltIn
    - https://www.builtin.com/
8. **Stack Overflow Jobs** – A platform focusing on tech-related roles, including opportunities for technical recruiters.
    - Stack Overflow Jobs
    - https://stackoverflow.com/jobs

Professional Networks and Communities

1. **LinkedIn Recruiter Groups** – Join groups like "Technical Recruiters" or "Talent Acquisition Professionals" to network with peers and get job leads.
    - LinkedIn Groups
    - https://www.linkedin.com/groups/
2. **Recruiting Brainfood** – A popular newsletter and community for recruiters, offering job opportunities and industry insights.
    - Recruiting Brainfood
    - https://www.recruitingbrainfood.com/

3. **ERE (Employee Referral Exchange)** – An online community for recruiters where you can find job postings and network with others in the field.
    - ERE
    - https://www.ere.net/
4. **Slack Communities** – Join Slack channels like "Tech Recruiter Nation" or "HR Open Source" for networking and job opportunities.
    - Tech Recruiter Nation Slack
    - https://join.slack.com/t/techrecruiternation
5. **Women in Tech Recruiter Groups** – Communities like "Women Who Code" have job boards and networking opportunities for women in tech recruiting.
    - Women Who Code
    - https://www.womenwhocode.com/

Company Career Pages

1. **Google Careers** – Google hires technical recruiters for its talent acquisition teams and has a dedicated career page.
    - Google Careers
    - https://careers.google.com/
2. **Amazon Jobs** – Frequently posts openings for technical recruiter roles, especially within AWS and other tech-focused teams.
    - Amazon Jobs
    - https://www.amazon.jobs/en/

3. **Meta Careers** – Meta (formerly Facebook) offers opportunities for technical recruiters to help scale their tech teams.
   - Meta Careers
   - https://www.metacareers.com/
4. **Microsoft Careers** – Microsoft recruits technical recruiters to support their growing technology teams globally.
   - Microsoft Careers
   - https://careers.microsoft.com/
5. **Tesla Careers** – Known for constant hiring, Tesla has ongoing opportunities for technical recruiters.
   - Tesla Careers
   - https://www.tesla.com/careers

Recruiter-Specific Job Boards

1. **Recruiter.com** – Specializes in recruiting roles, including tech recruiters, and offers job listings and resources.
   - Recruiter.com
   - https://www.recruiter.com/
2. **Talent.io** – A hiring platform focused on tech recruiting roles and connecting recruiters with tech companies.
   - Talent.io
   - https://www.talent.io/
3. **RecruitingDaily** – A resource hub for recruiters, including job postings for technical recruiting positions.
   - RecruitingDaily

- https://recruitingdaily.com/

Certifications & Courses to Enhance Your Profile

1. **LinkedIn Learning – Tech Recruiting Certification** – Offers online courses on technical recruiting best practices, sourcing, and industry knowledge.
    - LinkedIn Learning
    - https://www.linkedin.com/learning/

2. **Coursera – Technical Recruiting Specialization** – Online courses that focus on understanding technical roles and sourcing tech talent.
    - Coursera
    - https://www.coursera.org/

3. **TechRecruit Academy** – Provides specialized training and certifications for tech recruiters to stand out in the field.
    - TechRecruit Academy
    - https://www.techrecruit.io/

4. **Udemy – Technical Recruiting for Beginners** – Offers courses designed to build foundational skills in technical recruiting.
    - Udemy
    - https://www.udemy.com/

Recruitment Events & Conferences

1. **SourceCon** – A premier sourcing conference where recruiters can network and discover job opportunities.
    - SourceCon
    - https://www.sourcecon.com/

2. **HR Tech Conference** – Focuses on the latest HR technologies, providing networking opportunities and job leads for tech recruiters.

    - HR Tech Conference
    - https://www.hrtechnologyconference.com/

3. **Talent Acquisition Week** – A multi-day event that brings together talent acquisition professionals, offering insights and job opportunities.

    - Talent Acquisition Week
    - https://www.talentacquisitionweek.com/

4. **TechRecruit Conferences** – Dedicated conferences for technical recruiters to network, share knowledge, and explore career opportunities.

    - TechRecruit
    - https://www.techrecruit.io/

NOTES

www.ingramcontent.com/pod-product-compliance
Lightning Source LLC
Chambersburg PA
CBHW070208230526
45471CB00002B/871